Jewelry and Makeup

through History

by
Fiona MacDonald

GARETH STEVENS
GS
PUBLISHING
A Member of the WRC Media Family of Companies

Please visit our Web site at: www.garethstevens.com
For a free color catalog describing Gareth Stevens Publishing's
list of high-quality books and multimedia programs, call
1-800-542-2595 (USA) or 1-800-387-3178 (Canada).
Gareth Stevens Publishing's fax: (414) 332-3567.

Library of Congress Cataloging-in-Publication Data available upon request from publisher.
Fax (414) 336-0157 for the attention of the Publishing Records Department.

ISBN-10: 0-8368-6856-0 — ISBN-13: 978-0-8368-6856-2 (lib. bdg.)

This North American edition first published in 2007 by
Gareth Stevens Publishing
A Member of the WRC Media Family of Companies
330 West Olive Street, Suite 100
Milwaukee, Wisconsin 53212 USA

This edition copyright © 2007 by Gareth Stevens, Inc. Original edition copyright © 2006
by ticktock Entertainment Ltd. First published in Great Britain by ticktock Media Ltd.,
Unit 2 Orchard Business Centre, North Farm Road, Tunbridge Wells, Kent TN2 3XF.

Managing editor: Valerie J. Weber
Gareth Stevens editor: Gini Holland
Gareth Stevens art direction: Tammy West
Gareth Stevens designer: Kami Strunsee

Picture Credits (t=top, b=bottom, l=left, r=right, c=center)
Alamy: 22 all; Ancient Art and Architecture: 5 all, 11t, 11b, 16 all; Bridgeman Art Archive: 23 all;
CORBIS: 6b, 7 all, 12 all, 14t, 25 all, 26, 27t; Shutterstock: cover, 15t, 15b, 28-29 all;
ticktock Media Image Archive: title page all, 4 all, 13 all, 14-15, 20-21 all, 24 all, 27c 27b;
Werner Forman Archive: 18b, 19b, 5br, 6t, 8-9 all, 10t, 10b, 18t, 19t;
World Religions: 17 all.

Every effort has been made to trace the copyright holders, and we apologize in advance for any unintentional omission.
We would be pleased to insert the appropriate acknowledgements in any subsequent edition of this publication.

Printed in the United States of America

1 2 3 4 5 6 7 8 9 10 09 08 07 06

Table of Contents

Cover: Two women wear jewelry, while one woman helps the other put on her makeup.

Words that appear in the glossary are printed in
boldface type the first time they occur in the text.

Introduction

Some fantasies
are expressed with words
Others, with glances

004   DSERA

Young or old, male or female, most people decorate themselves in order to good and feel special. Some add eye-catching jewelry to their clothes and hair. Some wear makeup. Many hope makeup and jewelry will make them look great.

Makeup advertising is a billion-dollar industry. New products — modeled by naturally beautiful young women — offer the hope of beauty and glamour to customers.

Glamour

Makeup, also called **cosmetics**, can highlight attractive features on people's faces, such as their eyes, lips, and cheeks. Wearing makeup is supposed to attract others, linking it to **glamour** — an ancient word that originally meant magic spell. With makeup, people color their eyelids or create high arched eyebrows, part of a fashionable image. Makeup can help bring attention to people and make them feel special. By helping people feel that they look nice, makeup may boost some people's confidence or cheer them up when they feel sad.

Disguise

Makeup can also be used as a disguise. It can temporarily change a person's skin color or cover scars. People can simply wear makeup for amusement — for children's games, for putting on plays, or for costume parties. Face painting can change a face from plain to fancy.

Face painting is fun! It helps people pretend to be all sorts of different folks — or even animals — and to forget the everyday world for a while.

Special!

Jewelry is a sign that the wearer feels special. It reveals people's liking for pretty things or their **vanity** (high opinion of themselves). Jewelry often shows whether a person is married or single because people in many countries wear wedding or engagement rings. Jewelry can show a person's religious beliefs. Some Christians wear necklaces with **pendant** crosses, and some Hindus wear prayer beads. Many powerful people, such as chiefs and kings, wear splendid, valuable pieces of jewelry that display their wealth.

This African brass face pendant hangs from beads made from jade, two shades of turquoise, and Czech glass.

Work and Money

Traditionally, jewelry revealed the wearer's rank, occupation, or riches. In seventeenth-century China, top officials put jeweled **sheaths** on their long fingernails to show they were too high-ranking to do physical work. In eighteenth-century Europe, sailors were known by their gold rings in one ear. In North Africa and the Middle East, Bedouin women wore heavy silver jewelry — a safe, portable way for their families to store their savings.

Where does the word jewel *come from?*

These fingernail sheaths from seventeenth-century China are made of gold, silver, and turquoise.

The First Jewelry and Makeup

All over the world in all past ages, many men and women have worn jewelry. Many people have also painted themselves — and each other — with dramatic designs. Almost certainly, early people wore jewelry and makeup long before they started to wear clothes.

This mammoth bone pendant dates from 38,000 B.C. Found in the Czech Republic, it is decorated with incised patterns.

Stones and Bones

Jewelry may have originated more than 100,000 years ago. The first jewelry was made of natural objects including shells, feathers, and mammoth tusks. Later, **amber** and **jet** (a type of shiny black coal) were also made into jewelry. Later, people discovered how to shape beads from soft, **pliable** clay and decorate them with **incised** (scratched) patterns.

Natural Colors

Body paint has been found dating from about 50,000 B.C. The first people who wore makeup used natural substances, such as fruit juice to stain lips and cheeks red, ash to add shading around the eyes, and chalk and **ochre** (colored earth) to decorate the body. Mixed with fat or water, ochre created paint that could be spread over the body in patterns showing age, rank, or membership in a tribe. In some cultures, plant dyes

This Maori leader from New Zealand is wearing traditional facial tattoos.

were rubbed into cuts made in the skin to create permanent tattoos. This painful process was often a sign of honor awarded to members of powerful families or top warriors.

Stone and Metal Workers

Slowly, carefully, early people also learned how to cut and shape valuable stones and other hard materials, such as elephant ivory. They used stone axes to chip raw stone into a rough design. Then, they used grit or sand to smooth the surface. Finally, they used hand-powered bow drills to bore holes or engrave patterns.

This bronze axe is from the Mediterranean island of Crete and is over 5,000 years old.

Decorated All Over

Many early peoples used jewelry and makeup to decorate parts of their bodies. Some made headdresses, necklaces, armbands, earrings, nose rings, breast plates, or lip plugs (plates inserted under the lower lip). Many people tied decorations around their feet and legs, and some made pins from wood or bone to fasten their clothes together. Many people used body paints to add color to their looks.

Why did some people paint dead bodies red?

This man from Papua New Guinea is wearing a headdress and jewelry made from feathers, seeds, plant fibers, and shells.

Ancient Egypt and Its Neighbors

The ancient Egyptians were some of the first people to make jewelry from metal. They learned metal-working skills from nearby Anatolia (now Turkey) and West Asia, where **artisans** pioneered the production of copper, gold, and silver between about 7000 and 5000 B.C.

Eyes and Lips

Egyptian men and women wore makeup and rubbed perfumed ointment into their skin. Heavy eyeliner was their most important cosmetic. It was made from finely ground stone mixed with oil. Eyeliner might be green (containing **malachite**, a copper ore) or glittery black (based on a metallic material called **antimony**). Both were poisonous if eaten, but the Egyptians believed they gave protection from eye disease and also looked attractive. Egyptians tinted their lips with mixtures of fruits and herbs.

This fine *usekh* (jeweled collar necklace), found in the tomb of Pharaoh Tutankhamen (ruled from about 1361 to 1352 B.C.), is made of barrel-shaped gold and stone beads.

Bold and Bright

The favorite Egyptian metal was gold, which was brought to Egypt by traders and also paid to the pharaoh (king) as tribute from conquered peoples in Nubia (now Sudan). Egyptian jewelry included rings, bracelets, pendants, and wide, jeweled collars.

This famous painted bust of the Egyptian Queen Nefertiti was created in the fourteenth century B.C.

Ornamental Containers

Ordinary Egyptians stored their makeup in little pots of sun-dried clay. Wealthy Egyptians liked to store liquid makeup and perfumes in jewel-like jars of colored or patterned glass. Other valuable containers, carved from stone, were shaped like the god Bes, who was believed to increase fertility and protect households and families.

c. 3000 B.C. – 500

Magic Animals

Many pieces of Egyptian jewelry are shaped like animals or decorated with images of creatures, such as cobras and hawks. Egyptians thought these animal images had magical powers to bring good luck or divine help. They believed these images could bring people some of the animals' strength or beauty, bring good luck, or help call on the gods for protection.

Fine glass and stone containers like these made in the shape of the god Bes have been found in Egyptian tombs. Egyptians believed the dead would want go on wearing makeup in the afterlife.

Why were scarab beetles sacred to the Sun god?

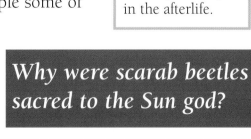

Scarabs (dung beetles) were sacred to Amun-Re, god of the life-giving Sun. Egyptians wore jewelry decorated with scarabs and carried these scarab-shaped lucky charms for protection.

Ancient Greece and Rome

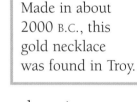

Greece was one of the first places in Europe to develop its own distinctive culture.

Treasure from Troy

When not at war, Greeks and their Trojan neighbors had peaceful trading contacts. Their trade goods included fabrics, foodstuffs, and gold. Trojan artisans made jewelry from pure sheet gold that they cut, hammered, or **engraved** to create earrings, necklaces, pendants, and **diadems**. Trojan styles and techniques influenced Greek artisans for many hundreds of years.

Made in about 2000 B.C., this gold necklace was found in Troy.

Myths and Makeup

Seal rings were used to show that a document was genuine. People pressed their rings into melted wax to leave their individual marks. These marks were often made in the form of a bird, a fish, or a magical-looking design.

After about 350 B.C., Greek artisans made magnificent bracelets, necklaces, pendants, and earrings. Most featured polished precious stones and braids of twisted gold wire. Decorations often included tiny molded scenes from Greek myths.

Greek men did not wear makeup. Greek women mixed soot, crushed earth, and herbs with olive oil to color lips, cheeks, and eyelids.

The ancient Romans ruled an empire that stretched from Scotland to Syria. Roman shopkeepers often used metals to create cosmetics, such as white lead

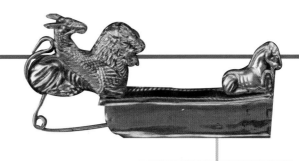

face powder. This powder created a fashionable, pale complexion, but, in large quantities, it could kill!

Wonderful Work

Romans wore more jewelry than anyone had ever worn before. Victorious armies and long-distance traders carried gold, silver, and precious stones to Rome. Jewelry makers moved to Rome from distant parts of the empire.

Roman jewelry styles were based on designs and techniques copied from the ancient Greeks and from the Etruscans, who lived in Italy before Rome grew powerful. Etruscan goldsmiths were extremely skillful. Their finest works include brooches decorated with tiny animals and patterned with **granulation**, which consists of rows of tiny metal balls. Roman jewelers pioneered many new techniques. These included cutting **cameos** and filling engraved lines with a black metal paste to create decorations called **niellos**.

> This Etruscan fibula (a fastening like a safety pin), made in about 500 B.C., is decorated with mythical creatures and edged with fine granulation.

Why did the ancient Greeks prize amethyst stones?

For Young and Old

Roman boys wore *bullas*, which were good luck lockets. Adult Roman men wore rings, bracelets, and medallions in large, chunky styles. Roman women preferred elaborate earrings, finger rings, and necklaces.

> This Roman boy's bulla hangs around his neck on a metal chain. Romans believed bullas protected boys and that it was bad luck to remove them.

Medieval Europe

Throughout southern Europe, Roman-style jewelry remained popular after A.D. 500, the start of the Middle Ages, or medieval period. In the north and east, Roman styles replaced local designs. Women continued to wear makeup, but the fast-growing Christian church taught that cosmetics were sinful. By A.D. 1000, makeup and body paint were out of favor in all Christian lands.

A warrior's face, with goggle eyes, peers out from this gold-and-silver pin. It was found in an Anglo-Saxon grave and was made in about A.D. 550.

Anglo-Saxons and Vikings

In Britain, Germany, and Scandinavia, jewelers created magnificent brooches of gold, silver, and bronze. They designed these pins to fasten cloaks and other clothing, so brooches were useful as well as beautiful. **Anglo-Saxons** decorated jewelry with braided wire, **filigree** (lacy twisted metal), polished precious stones, and brightly colored **enamel** (layer of glass). Viking jewelers preferred solid metal shaped by hammering, twisting, carving, and **casting** techniques.

Charms, Necklaces, and Rings

Favorite Viking jewelry included **amulets** (lucky charms) and huge, heavy metal necklaces and arm rings. These pieces were often given to warriors by Viking chiefs as rewards for bravery in battle. Viking jewelry for women featured large brooches and necklaces strung with imported treasures, such as glass beads from Germany, coins from western Asia, or amber from the eastern shores of the Baltic Sea.

This Viking necklace was made of carefully shaped amber beads, probably in about A.D. 900. The original bead string has rotted away.

This early medieval brooch from Wales in Great Britain was made in the eighth century.

Christian Symbols

After about A.D. 1000, medieval jewelry was often made in the shape of Christian symbols or decorated with portraits of saints. Medieval people also liked jewelry in non-religious designs. They wore souvenir pins to show that they had traveled to distant places and **heraldic** badges to display their ancestry or loyalty to their lord. They also gave and wore jewelry as a sign of love.

Which jewel was thought to protect wearers from plague?

Jeweled Clothes

By the end of the Middle Ages, in about A.D. 1500, rich peoples' clothes were often trimmed with real gold and silver embroidery. Wealthy women wore **girdles** decorated with pearls. Powerful men dressed in jewel-studded buckles and heavy gold chains. Ordinary people could not afford such luxury. Instead, they added cheap iron pins and brooches to their clothes.

This tapestry (wall hanging) was woven in Flanders (now Belgium) in about A.D. 1500. It shows wealthy women wearing jewelry and richly jeweled clothes.

Asia

Throughout the vast continent of Asia, many different styles of jewelry and makeup were created. Many designs, shaped by local customs and beliefs as well as by local materials, are still in use in Asia today.

"Shaking When Walking"

In ancient China, jewelry was traditionally sewn onto clothes. Chinese hooks and buckles were made from bone, ivory, and bronze. Hairpins, used to fasten women's long hair, often had jingling pendants attached, so they were known as *pu yao,* or "shaking when walking." Traditional Chinese jewelry did not feature any precious stones except smooth green **jade**, the symbol of wisdom, courage, and long life. Carved into beads and decorations, jade was sewn onto clothing.

These two-pronged Chinese hairpins were made of cut and twisted silver in about A.D. 800.

Holy Signs, Precious Stones

Many of the world's finest gems have been found in India. Worn in large quantities by rich women in the past, they often covered the body like a second skin. Married Hindu women and holy men still wear a red dot on the forehead, which is said to be the site of a mystical "third eye" that brings spiritual understanding. For good luck, many Muslim brides cover their hands and feet with **henna** patterns before their weddings.

Ground-up leaves of henna plants stain the skin a brownish red. Henna patterns last for about three weeks.

14

Prayer Beads

In western and central Asia, many Muslim men still carry strings of traditional *mesbah* (prayer beads). These have been used since the eighth century to help focus the mind on religion. As worshippers run the beads through their fingers, they repeat the words *Subhana Allah* (glory to God). To reflect their religious value, mesbah are often made from semiprecious stones, such as amber, turquoise, or coral.

Traditionally, prayer beads were strung in groups of thirty-three, sixty-six, or ninety-nine and finished with a silken tassel.

> *Why did so many people wear makeup for celebrations?*

Decorative Details

In ancient Japan, most people did not wear jewelry. As in China, the only acceptable ornaments were hairpins and clothes fastenings. Men wore decorative **netsuke** (toggles) to secure their robes and hung beautifully carved **inro** (pill boxes) from their belts. Ordinary people did not wear cosmetics, but male actors and **geishas** (elegant female entertainers) wore heavy makeup to hide their ordinary selves and take on different roles when they performed.

Two geishas wear makeup in Kyoto, Japan.

I n Africa, jewelry, makeup, and body decorations all featured bold, dramatic designs. Many patterns still have meanings based on ancient rituals and history, and they are also used in other crafts, such as textiles.

Desert Silver

In North Africa, silver was the chosen metal for jewelry. North Africans combined silver with large semiprecious stones, especially amber, or reused silver coins. Among nomadic peoples, like the Tuareg of the Sahara Desert, jewelry was a way of safely storing and carrying family wealth. Jewelry was also often believed to have a protective value. Tuareg artisans made amulets in many different shapes to be worn by men and women. Camel's-eye designs symbolized power, jackal tracks stood for cunning, and circles were signs of fertility. Amber was said to cure illness.

This Tuareg silver necklace is from the late nineteenth centu

Heavy Metal

In the rest of Africa, gold was the preferred precious metal. It was usually hammered into bracelets, necklaces, and rings, but West African goldsmiths were also expert at casting elaborate ornaments by pouring melted gold into finely detailed molds. Copper was also a popular metal, especially for women's jewelry. In southern Africa, women wore bracelets, anklets, and armbands made from decorated copper wire incised with geometric patterns.

This unique gold ring was made in Ghana in about 1900.

Paint and Patterns

Ordinary African people could not afford precious metals. They made necklaces, belts, and bracelets from leather, bone, and stone. They also painted striking designs on bodies and faces. Body paint was mostly worn when taking part in special ceremonies, such as one to announce that a young boy or girl had passed from childhood to adulthood. Scarification (patterns of scars made on the skin) displayed membership of a warrior brotherhood or powerful family clan.

This village elder from Sudan is shown wearing traditional scarification that is highlighted with a mud paste across his forehead.

How did teenage Zulu girls send love letters?

Beautiful Beads

The first glass beads in Africa were made by the ancient Egyptians over 3,000 years ago. Farther south, African peoples also made beads of bone, stone, and clay. Later, they purchased colored glass beads from European traders. Beads were used to make necklaces, belts, anklets, and bracelets and to decorate other personal items, such as hats and bags. Often, beads carried a special meaning. Among the Masai people (in what is now Kenya) the number of bead necklaces a woman wore showed whether she was married or not, how many children she had, and how rich her family was. Among Zulu people (in present-day South Africa), different colored beads sent coded messages: red for anger, blue for love, black for danger, brown for despair, and green for peace.

The ancient tradition of beadwork still continues today, as shown by this Zulu woman from South Africa.

17

Early Americas

N ative American jewelry ranged from plain and simple to rich and elaborate. It was made from many different materials in styles reflecting local customs, traditions, and religious beliefs.

Feathers and Flowers

The Maya lived in the rain forests of Mesoamerica. They were ruled by kings who claimed godlike powers. Mayan royalty wore rich robes and wonderful jewelry — headdresses, bracelets, belts, earrings, and necklaces hung with heavy pendants or plaques. Favorite materials included gold, jade, and shells. Designs were often based on rain-forest animals and flowers.

This Mayan container — holding incense burned during religious ceremonies — is decorated with the image of a god-king wearing heavy, elaborate jewels.

Life and Death

The Aztecs of Mexico demanded gold as **tribute**, or taxes, from the peoples they conquered. Aztec jewelry was made from this gold, along with feathers, turquoise, rock crystal, and **obsidian** (volcanic glass). By law, jewelry could be worn only by rulers and nobles. Often, it portrayed the Aztecs' guardian gods. The Aztecs believed that these gods would destroy the world unless they were offered human sacrifices.

This skull-shaped Aztec pendant is beautifully made from thin sheets of hammered gold.

This necklace was made by the Fox Indians, who lived between the Great Lakes and Great Plains regions of North America. The necklace features fur, turquoise beads, and grizzly bear claws.

Teeth and Claws

Early Native American people made jewelry from shiny orange copper. They cut and hammered copper beads, pendants, plaques, bracelets, and earrings. Favorite designs included birds, snakes, and human hands. Native Americans also used other natural materials, such as turquoise, coral, shells, porcupine quills, beaks, feathers, animal teeth, and claws. Jewelry made from parts of fierce wild animals, such as eagles or grizzly bears, was worn by important people only. Such jewelry was a sign of high status and suggested that the wearers shared in the animals' dignity, courage, and power.

Sacred Paint

Native Americans wore face and body paint for important occasions. These included funerals, when a dead body was respectfully "dressed" in color, and fearful, dangerous times, such as setting out for war. Each Native nation had its own paint colors and patterns. Red, the symbol of life-giving blood, was a favorite color of many tribes. Patterns were often copied from nature, and many featured the mighty shining sun.

What were the "sweat of the sun" and the "tears of the moon"?

This Sioux warrior, painted in the mid-nineteenth century, is wearing a feather headdress, beadwork, and red face paint.

19

Europe produces little gold and silver and few precious stones. After A.D. 1500, however, European explorers reached lands where both could be found in large quantities. Ships brought Indian diamonds, Sri Lankan sapphires, Burmese rubies, Arabian pearls, and South American emeralds, gold, and silver back to Europe.

Jewelry and Art

Rich Europeans paid top artists and designers to create masterpiece jewelry for them. Jewelry for women included long necklaces, hair ornaments, pendants, and rings set with large, precious stones. Men also wore rings, together with jeweled belts, collars, and big medallions on their hats.

After about A.D. 1550, miniature portraits were set in gold, surrounded by jewels and then worn on the chest like a brooch.

Dressed to Impress

On state occasions, rival kings and princes all tried to display the most magnificent jewels.

They also paid for artists to record their splendid appearances, weighed down by jewel-studded crowns, weapons, **scepters**, miniature portraits, and robes. For public appearances, women — and some men — wore makeup and rich, heavy perfumes.

Queen Elizabeth I of England (who ruled from 1558 to 1603) had copies of her portraits sent all around the country to impress the people she ruled. She is seen here wearing white face makeup and astonishing jewels and holding a scepter.

New Styles, Lower Prices

Rich jewelry remained popular in the seventeenth century, but designs changed dramatically. People preferred graceful, flowing shapes and styles based on plants and flowers. Makeup became more natural looking and was worn by many more women. Often, they made skin lotions and lip tints at home and dusted their faces with fine white flour. Fine jewels remained extremely expensive and were for kings, queens, and nobles only. Middle-ranking people, however, could now afford smaller, more modest pieces, such as gold wedding rings. These had been worn by the rich since ancient Egyptian times but had been too costly for ordinary couples.

1500 — 1750

Glitter and Sparkle

In about 1550, and again in 1640, new technologies were developed in the Netherlands and France to improve the appearance of imported precious stones. Instead of simply polishing stones, jewelry makers began to cut them with brilliant **facets**, or angled surfaces. Faceted stones reflect light back at viewers, glittering and sparking as the wearer moves.

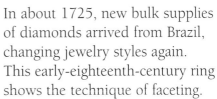

In about 1725, new bulk supplies of diamonds arrived from Brazil, changing jewelry styles again. This early-eighteenth-century ring shows the technique of faceting.

When did engagement rings first become fashionable?

Western World 1750–1900

After 1750, machines replaced manpower in many industries. Fine jewelry was still created — slowly and carefully — by expert artisans. Now, however, cheap mass-produced jewelry was made on machines. Makeup and body-care products were also produced in factories.

Lockets for Locks

As ideas about family, society, and politics all changed, new kinds of jewelry appeared. Mourning jewelry was especially popular in Britain, echoing the sentimental feeling of the Victorian era. Made of somber materials, such as dark **ebony** or black jet, lockets often bore the name or portrait of the deceased. Sometimes, a lock of the dead person's hair was also included.

A mourning locket, made in about 1800, shows a woman crying beside a burial **urn** (a container for ashes) and weeping willow leaves, which are a traditional symbol of grief.

Royal Display

Kings, queens, and nobles continued to wear large amounts of fabulous jewelry. Expert jewelry makers, such as the Fabergé family of St. Petersburg, Russia, specialized in jewelry and luxurious objects for royalty throughout Europe. These objects included pretty but useless items, such as jeweled false Easter eggs.

This Fabergé egg and necklace were made in about 1900.

Gold and Diamonds

The United States had no royalty, but the Tiffany family of New York designed new ways of setting high-quality precious stones for members of rich families to wear. Their products included solitaires — large stones, chosen for their brilliance, set alone on rings. Gold now came from California, where it was discovered in 1848, and from new mines in Australia and Africa. Rich

The success of the Kimberly diamond mines (*above in 1888*) encouraged thousands of prospectors to flock to South Africa in search of riches.

deposits of diamonds were also found in South Africa during the 1870s. As a result, gold and diamond jewelry became very fashionable.

What is the largest diamond ever discovered on Earth?

For Celebrities

Fashionable jewelry-making companies also supplied diamonds to glamorous celebrities, such as actresses and opera stars. These women were famous and talented but shunned by leaders of "polite" society who disapproved of their clothes, makeup, and behavior.

Throughout the nineteenth century, respectable men and women stopped using perfume or cosmetics, except for faint flower scents and invisible skin cream. Colored lips and cheeks, dyed hair, strong scents, and powdered faces were said to be signs of immorality.

This painting, *Cinderella and Her Wicked Sisters,* by Emile Meyer, illustrates how the excessive use of makeup was frowned upon in the Victorian era.

1750 — 1900

People still give jewelry as presents or love tokens. It is offered as prizes in competitions and as rewards for hard work or good behavior. It is handed down from one generation to another to preserve and encourage happy memories.

At Sikh weddings in India, a close male relative puts bangles on the bride's wrists. She is supposed to keep them on for forty days to bring luck.

Making Faces

Today, makeup is worn by many millions of women. For many, it is part of their identity. Makeup also creates a "face" for people in the public eye, from politicians to entertainers. Beauty care is now a vast industry,

A model has lipstick applied just before a fashion shoot in Hong Kong, 2003.

controlled by **multinational** companies. They offer consumers countless new products in changing colors and **textures**. Some **formulations** are modern and high-tech. Others are based on natural and herbal ingredients. Today, makeup can look fashionable, natural, messy, startling, or chic.

Hollywood Style

By the 1930s, movies were the most popular form of mass entertainment in the Western world. Fashionable film stars wore art deco jewelry and dramatic makeup both on and off screen. In France, companies such as L'Oreal (founded in 1909) pioneered new, scientific ways of manufacturing cosmetics. In the United States in the 1930s, Max Factor created special makeup for film photography — and won a prestigious Oscar award. Cosmetics were widely advertised in popular new women's magazines and once again became respectable.

Actress Ginger Rogers applies makeup in her Hollywood dressing room in 1933.

Real Plastic, Fake Jewels

The first plastic that could be molded easily was invented in 1909 by Leo Baekeland, a Belgian-born chemist living in the United States. It was widely used for jewelry and for other decorative items, such as buckles and buttons. Plastic could be cast (poured into molds) to mass-produce fancy shapes that would have taken hours or days to carve by hand. It could also be colored to imitate coral, turquoise, tortoiseshell, and many other natural materials. At around the same time, scientists experimented with ways of creating precious stones. In 1900, French chemist August Verneuil invented a way of making rubies that is still used today.

These colorful plastic buttons were made in 1910 in a wide variety of shapes.

Western World 1950–2000

I n the late twentieth century, expensive jewelry featured big, bold shapes and angular designs and used new materials, such as gold flakes set in plastic or titanium. **Synthetic** jewelry was also invented, while many other pieces were mass-produced or imported.

Discreet or Dramatic?

During the 1950s, a mature, sophisticated look was fashionable. Most women used discreet face-powder and **matte** (non-shiny) red lipstick to appear neat and elegant. A few bleached their hair, used bright red lipstick, and covered their faces with so-called peach-skin foundation in sexy film-star style. Most women wore jewelry that included simple wedding rings, clip-on earrings, jeweled pins, and pearl necklaces. More daring women often wore flashy designs called costume jewelry, which usually featured bright gold with big, colored stones.

Glitter, Gloss, and Blusher

By the 1960s, most people preferred a much younger look. New makeup ingredients made fresh effects possible, including huge, childlike eyes with long, spiky lashes, pale complexions, and white or pale pink lipstick. Flakes of minerals, such as mica, made eye shadow glittery. Lip gloss and blusher gave faces sheer, shiny color. Jewelry in the 1960s was influenced by traditional Indian and African designs.

Film star Diana Dors, shown here in 1953, wore vivid makeup.

The famous 1960s model Twiggy wears pale lipstick and spiky false eyelashes.

Piercing, Paint, and Chains

For most of the twentieth century, toiletries for men were limited to soap, hair cream, and sometimes after-shave lotion. By the 1970s and 1980s, young men were experimenting with products, such as cleanser and hair spray. "Glam rock" musicians made eye makeup popular; other young men aimed for a bronzed, surfer look. Rival music and fashion trends, such as heavy metal and punk, featured face paint together with body piercing, tattooing, and massive metal rings and chains.

This woman pictured in the 1990s wears multiple rings and facial piercings.

Synthetic Stones

Throughout the twentieth century, scientists continued to experiment with making precious stones in laboratories and with treating natural stones to increase their value. Cubic zirconium, a cheap diamond substitute, was created 1977. Dull, white topaz was exposed to radiation to turn it a dazzling bright blue. New, flexible and transparent plastics were also used for cheap jewelry. They could be covered with shiny paint to look like metal or be cast in faceted shapes, like real jewels.

Why can tattooing and body piercing be dangerous?

This synthetic gemstone was made to imitate more expensive jewels.

Global Styles Today

Today, there no single style of fashionable jewelry. Showy, extravagant items are mostly worn by celebrities to display their sudden success. Some designs, like wedding rings, are worn all over the world. Others continue to be worn mainly in the countries in which they are made.

Signs of God

Many Christians wear cross pendants or pins in the shape of a fish. Jews often wear six-pointed Stars of David, and Muslims have pendants carved with the holy name of Allah (God). These believers usually treasure religious jewelry more for its spiritual value than its material worth.

Religious jewelry is designed to remind wearers of God.

Where did the name bling bling come from?

Bling Bling

In the early 2000s, glittering chains, rings, pendants, and buckles became popular among hip-hop musicians and their male fans. They were made of real (or fake) diamonds set in heavy silver or gold. A few were studded with flashing, battery-powered **LEDs.** This lavish jewelry is known as *bling bling*. It symbolizes a love of money, a defiant attitude, youth, energy, glamour, and pride.

Jewelry for Joy

Jewels still play a part in many traditional ceremonies. These range from state festivals, like coronations, to family occasions, such as weddings or bar mitzvahs (Jewish coming-of-age celebrations).

Rapper Won G wears a heavy bling-bling chain in 2002.

People still give jewelry as presents or love tokens. It is offered as prizes in competitions and as rewards for hard work or good behavior. It is handed down from one generation to another to preserve and encourage happy memories.

At Sikh weddings in India, a close male relative puts bangles on the bride's wrists. She is supposed to keep them on for forty days to bring luck.

Making Faces

Today, makeup is worn by many millions of women. For many, it is part of their identity. Makeup also creates a "face" for people in the public eye, from politicians to entertainers. Beauty care is now a vast industry, controlled by **multinational** companies. They offer consumers countless new products in changing colors and **textures**. Some **formulations** are modern and high-tech. Others are based on natural and herbal ingredients. Today, makeup can look fashionable, natural, messy, startling, or chic.

A model has lipstick applied just before a fashion shoot in Hong Kong, 2003.

Glossary

amber fossilized tree resin used in jewelry

amulets lucky charms

Anglo-Saxons people who migrated from North Germany to Britain about A.D. 500

antimony a dark gray metal

artisans people who make finely crafted objects, such as jewelry and pottery

cameos gems, stones, or shells carved with faces or scenes in such a way that the first layers show up in different colors than the second layers

casting shaping by pouring hot metal into a mold

cosmetics another name for makeup

diadems decorative headbands

ebony dark, precious, tropical wood

enamel a thin layer of colored glass fused (bonded by heating) onto metal

engraved cut into a flat surface

facets angled surfaces cut onto stones

filigree a type of decoration made of fine, twisted wire

formulations mixtures prepared according to specified formulas

geishas elegant female entertainers in Japan

girdles in historic times, belts or bands of cloth worn around the waist

glamour the quality of being attractive, fascinating, and sophisticated

granulation a type of jewelry decoration made from tiny metal balls

henna a reddish-brown dye made from crushed plant leaves of the henna plant

heraldic patterns or symbols showing membership of a noble family or loyalty to a lord

incised cut or scratched into a surface

inro decorated, usually compartmented, pillboxes made in Japan

jade a smooth, hard green type of stone

jet hard, shiny black coal

LEDs an acronym for light emitting diode, a semiconductor used to light up things like watches

malachite a green, soft, copper-based semiprecious stone

matte having a smooth and non-shiny surface

multinational a company, corporation, or other kind of organization that operates in more than two countries

netsuke carved, decorated toggles used to fasten clothes in Japan

niellos decorations made by cutting lines into a metallic surface and then filling the lines in with black paste

obsidian shiny black glass produced by hardened lava from volcanoes

ochre tannish-yellow colored earth used to color paints

pavé jewels set so that they flatly cover a metal base

pendant a jewelry item than hangs around the neck from a string, cord, or chain

pliable easy to bend; flexible

scepters sticks or batons held as a sign of authority, usually by royalty or a religious authority figure

sheaths close-fitting coverings, such as narrow dresses, knife-holders worn on belts, or fingernail extensions

synthetic not a product of nature; created artificially

textures the appearance and feel of something, as in rough or smooth

tribute tax paid by conquered peoples

urn container, often used for the ashes of a dead, cremated person.

vanity excessive pride or an unreasonably high opinion of oneself

Answers

Page 5: from an ancient Roman word meaning "plaything"

Page 7: because red is the color of life-sustaining blood

Page 9: because scarab beetles came out of the dirt and seemed to live forever, they represented eternal returns to life, like the Sun returning daily to the sky

Page 11: they believed amethysts would prevent drunkenness

Page 13: bezoar stone — a natural substance found in the digestive system of goats! It did not work.

Page 15: for protection because traditionally, celebrations were beleived to be dangerous times when envious evil spirits might attack happy people

Page 17: they sent beaded trinkets

Page 19: names for gold and silver used by the Incan people of South America

Page 21: in about A.D. 1500, in Italy; they were often made of silver

Page 23: the Cullinan Diamond, which was dug up in the new mines of South Africa in 1905 and weighed more than 1 pound/almost .5 kilogram

Page 24: by dropping chemicals through a flame heated to a staggering 3,600 °F/ 2,000 °C — or more

Page 27: unless sterile (or disposable) equipment is used, they can spread dangerous infections, including HIV

Page 28: from Jamaica in the Caribbean, these words described the jingling sound that heavy, swinging jewelry often makes

Index